LOVE NOTES FROM HEAVEN

CYNTHIA HIGHTOWER

Love Notes from Heaven

Trilogy Christian Publishers A Wholly Owned Subsidary of Trinity Broadcasting Network

2442 Michelle Drive Tustin, CA 92780

Cover design by: Kristy Swank

For information about special discounts for bulk purchases, please contact Trilogy Christian Publishing.

Manufactured in the United States of America

10 9 8 7 6 5 4 3 2 1

Library of Congress Cataloging-in-Publication Data is available.

ISBN: 978-1-68556-701-9

E-ISBN: 78-1-68556-702-6

DEDICATION

I dedicate this book, *Love Notes from Heaven*: Living in the Whisper of God to my beloved brother, John and his precious wife, Christie. Without their help, I would not have been able to write and publish this book.

Table of Contents

FOREWORD

Through the years, have collected spiritual experiences that could not be explained as natural phenomena. I have treasured the remembrance of these happenings as jewels in a treasure chest. They are valued above earthly possessions.

In connecting with other Christians, I have discovered that some of these experiences have been known by others, as well. I have shared some of these spiritual happenings with family, friends, church members, and more recently, with friends I have become close to on social media.

In collecting the testimonies for this book, I have listened to the observances of close friends and, more recently, to acquaintances I have encountered while writing this account of God's sweet flow of communication with His creation, the flawed but greatly loved human race.

Their stories have inspired me as I have endeavored to clearly document their accounts of the Holy Spirit moving in their lives. There is something about coming into contact with Christians who tell of their spiritual encounters. When I bump into these people, something begins to stir within the core of my being. As you read, may your spirit catch the fire of the Holy Spirit as a candle burning within. This is my desire.

I have included a few scriptures, all from the King James Version.

Love and blessings,

Cynthia

Love Notes from Heaven

When I wrote an article for social media and released it to several Christian groups, I was amazed with the response. The article was about God communicating with His people through releasing fragrances. As I researched this subject, I kept running into people who mentioned other supernatural experiences as they shared their testimonies.

When the Holy Spirit begins to move, there are various manifestations of the Spirit that rush forth, and they begin to bump into each other. It is hard to isolate them. It's as hard to keep them apart as keeping lively children in a school yard separated once recess has begun. Therefore, you will see different phenomena flowing together in the testimonies, so the format of this book is like a flowing river. It is time to get in your canoe and flow with me in this stream of consciousness river. This river flows, telling of the perpetual goodness of God.

Through the years, I have collected spiritual experiences that could not be explained in the natural. Even as Mary, the mother of Jesus, pondered in her heart, I have held onto some things and pondered them in my heart.

In connecting with other Christians, I have discovered that some of these experiences have been known by others, as well. It has been like putting pieces of a puzzle together to get the big picture.

As I have learned about the various means of communication, I have noticed a common pattern. They have carried the benevolent nature of God. These communications have been sent to benefit the Covenant children who are greatly loved by their Heavenly Father.

Therefore, I have begun to call them "Love Notes from Heaven." Some of God's love notes are lengthy, such as the sixty-six books of the Bible and the beauty and vastness of the universe. Almighty God has written some extensive love letters to humanity.

The testimonies in this book are more like short, passionate love notes. They are love notes from heaven. Each one was written by God's own hand. The stories are love notes to the Covenant children, straight from Father's heart.

Father chases us down to bless us at times. Even as our lives become loaded down with the cares of this world, He still attempts to communicate with us to give us clues about how to navigate on the journey of life. One example of this is when God tries to speak to a person all day long, but the person is too preoccupied to perceive the messages God is sending. After numerous attempts to communicate with that person but not being acknowledged, Father deposits a vivid dream the person cannot forget. When the conscious mind shuts down, the Lord speaks to the subconscious mind, and upon awakening, the dream is acknowledged.

> *For God speaketh once, yea twice, yet man perceiveth it not. In a dream, in a vision of the night, when sleep falleth upon men, in slumberings upon the bed; then he openeth the ears of men and sealeth their instruction.*

Job 33:14–16

For years, I had interpreted my own dreams as the meanings of spiritual dreams came almost immediately upon awakening. After my daughter had married, God gave me a dream of three tigers in a field. They were young, beautiful, fierce, and confident. They all looked the same, but I knew that one was a female. The three tigers walked in a

8

ircle out in the field, and they walked in unity. Because they were tigers, I did not want to get too close, but as I walked away from the field, I was comforted in knowing they were not too far away.

When I woke up, I thought, *What was that all about?* Then suddenly, I knew! These were my three grandchildren who would be born into the world. Three grandchildren were born in the following years—the girl, then the two boys. I had interpreted this dream suddenly and accurately, not knowing that I would be interpreting about a thousand dreams each year in the last five and a half years.

When talking to a woman in my church, I learned that she had seen her youngest three grandchildren before they had been conceived, just as I had, but she did not see them in symbols. She had seen them literally as they would look in every detail.

You may wonder why God would give grandmothers dreams of their grandchildren. I believe one reason is to assure families of the destinies of their young ones. I have heard so many saying, "They have all they need; they don't need another one; they have a boy and a girl, and their family is complete." When God wants to send another child into a family, He sometimes announces their destinies. Just as Mary and Elizabeth prophesied over two special ministries about to be birthed, the children in our families may have their births announced, as well.

When my daughter was seventeen, I was praying about her life and the family she would have in the future, and as I prayed, God gave me a word of knowledge that she would have three children. I did not share this word of knowledge with her because some things should not be spoken out immediately. Even as Mary pondered things in her heart, I held this word of three grandchildren close to me. When my daughter was twenty and involved with her studies and activities, she came home after the semester and shared with me how she would like to marry and have a family someday. Then she said, "I would like to have at least three children, and I would like to have both sons and daughters." There has been a lot of confirmation about these children of destiny.

I have been surprised by the stories I have heard in Sunday school classes as I have moved to different towns through the years. These stories of supernatural happenings have come from those with varying denominational backgrounds since small towns may have only one Sunday school still open. Through the years, I have met some ordinary people who have had extraordinary, supernatural experiences.

I was in my mid-twenties when I began to hear that some Christians had supernatural encounters beyond my experience. It was interesting, but I told God that I did not want to see any of the "scary stuff." He heard my prayer, and He has filtered out the things I did not want to see and hear. However, when I have been in environments that were not safe, I have sensed this, even when my friends who were with me did not sense the danger.

Several years ago, more dreams and visions were being told to me. They were not telling me sweet dreams or funny dreams. I was hearing scary, apocalyptic dreams. Wherever I went, the dreamer found me! I was not having the apocalyptic dreams, but I was hearing them. Some of the most ordinary people in the world would track me down to tell me their vivid dreams and visions that they could not forget.

I could not travel far enough to get away from these people. I could settle in some of the most remote places on earth, and the dreamers would appear. At first, I considered this to be something to overcome, and trusted God to give me strength and patience to endure. In time, I began to receive peace to be able to hear these messages from the visionaries

One day, when I had traveled about a hundred fifty miles to see my beloved aunts, we were in a small café enjoying our visit. My cell phone rang, and another relative gave a desperate account of a vision she had just seen with her natural eyes. I was trying to calm her as she was telling of the catastrophic event she had just witnessed, as I tried to remain poised while my family was visiting at the table. At this point, I was becoming more accustomed to hearing these things. In recent years, I have learned to advise praying for more insight and praying for God's mercy to be poured out, except for apocalyptic dreams showing Bible prophecy being fulfilled, and even as prophecy is being fulfilled, I still believe God's hand of mercy can still be extended to individuals.

I hear people saying, "Why does God allow things like this to happen to people?" I believe God sends warnings, but we have not gotten proficient at cracking the codes, which become much simpler to understand the longer I am involved with interpreting them. I like to help people understand their dreams and visions. Understanding the dream brings peace to the dreamer, and they are more likely to be able to know how to work with God in the scenario that is about to unfold. A warning is a love note because it may serve to stop a dangerous event, lessen its effects, or prevent some people from being harmed by it.

Before I knew very much about visions, I kept seeing the face of a man I had only been introduced to one time and had no further contact with him. I was having this vision with my spiritual eyes, in my "mind's eye," as they say. Most of my visions have been with spiritual eyes, not my natural eyes. However, I have learned to take these visions seriously. When I was seeing this man's face, I was under stress and not on a spiritual mountaintop. I dismissed seeing this face as a mere curiosity. I wish I had prayed for him. Later, I found out that he had committed suicide. We learn from our mistakes, but I am also determined to teach from my mistakes. There is no need for all of us to make the same mistakes. In retrospect, I wonder how many were given warnings about this man's early death.

As I began to receive more reports of dreams and visions, I knew that they were from God. Knowing this, I felt a responsibility to try to listen and understand. After all, it was obvious that Heavenly Father was trying to communicate with us in these dreams and visions.

Most visionaries (a term that I sometimes use to describe those who receive information from the Lord in dreams, visions, and other means of revelation) are intercessors. The insight they are given from the dreams and visions does increase their effectiveness in prayer. Some visionaries deliver information to teams of intercessors.

Most dreams originate from the subconscious mind of the dreamer. Dream interpreters usually call these "soul dreams" because they originate within the soul/mind of the dreamer. They present a way for the human mind to process thoughts and feelings that have been repressed, and they are important in maintaining emotional health in the individual. The enemy occasionally sends his poison dart dreams, and these dreams may give clues about his destructive plans. Those who have dabbled in the occult or participated in a life of sin will have more of those dark dreams. They often give the dreamer clues about what to pray against. Canceling the plans of the enemy in Jesus' name is a positive outcome of such dreams.

Dreams that have captured much of my attention are spiritual dreams, also called "God dreams." These are dreams sent by our loving and patient Heavenly Father to inform, guide, correct, and direct. Interpreting these God dreams has become a quest. I have interpreted over five thousand dreams in the last five and a half years. After stumbling into a dream interpretation group on social media, I discovered I could interpret, and the rest is history. Our highly intelligent Ancient of Days enjoys spinning a riddle in a quest to communicate with His creation. If He stated every communication directly, the message might come so abruptly that the receiver of the communication might not receive it. I seek to unravel the riddles day after day.

One of the best things in accepting this ministry of interpreting for the visionaries is that the fear has left. (I also interpret for some of the general population, even though their dreams are more likely to be soul dreams.) Even when I hear details that once would have had me wishing I could find a better place to hide, I am now able to manage the details rather matter-of-factly. And it gives me a sense of accomplishment when I see peace settle over the dreamer. Dreams tend to be more symbolic than visions, and knowing the meaning sets the dreamer's mind at ease. I have seen deliverance and emotional healing follow interpretations, as well. When dreams are interpreted for a time, the dreamer may begin to develop emotionally after years of being held back from developing normally. This is one of the benefits of interpreting soul dreams for those who are willing to listen to what their own subconscious mind is telling them. Some of the dreamers are receiving treatment from professional counselors because they need therapy in addition to dream interpretations.

When I have interviewed people for this book, they have been from diverse backgrounds. Some have had one memorable, supernatural experience in a long life, and it has become a treasured memory that has adorned their lifelong relationship with the Lord as a choice jewel. Others I have interviewed have had numerous experiences. In some cases, there is almost a perpetual flow of supernatural occurrences.

Some of those I have interviewed have had many visions and deep, spiritual insight, but they do not wish to claim ministry titles. These individuals have told me, "I want to be available to God wherever He needs me." Others readily claim ministry titles, such as prophetic artist, prophetic intercessor, seer, evangelist, etc. I believe the titles are a matter of preference. I have met some spiritually perceptive Christians who claim no titles at all.

Repeatedly, I have been told of when they first began to experience receiving information in the supernatural realm. Some were very young when they began to receive visions with their natural eyes. They were too young to have reached the age of accountability, but apparently, God does not always wait until they have made the choice to receive salvation. Several have mentioned the age of four or five as the time when they saw their first visions. Others have told me that as soon as they received salvation, the dreams and visions began immediately or very soon afterward.

Their occupations are more diverse than their ministry titles. This is a sprinkling of some of the occupations I have discovered: a licensed professional counselor, college professors, a high school economics teacher, a grocery store checker, an okra farmer in Africa, a retired junior high principal, a refugee, who has not yet mentioned her job title, a night watchman, and housewives. Through the years, I have noticed that many of the spiritually gifted women love to be housewives if they have a choice. They like to have time to hear from the Lord.

This book is written from interviews with women, but I have noticed that spiritually gifted men have career preferences, as well. One bi-vocational male pastor told my mother that he liked to mow lawns to supplement his small pastor's salary, saying, "When I am outside doing yard work, I can keep my mind on the Lord." Another man who was an intercessor and liked to spend many hours a day in prayer asked God to show him how to earn a living with many ours left over for prayer. God showed him that he could advertise metal buildings in the newspaper and mark the price up a bit. He sold enough buildings to pay his living expenses while he spent most of his hours in prayer. Being a serious intercessor, bearing the burdens of others is a consuming ministry, and there are many faithful ones who go about their work, mostly unnoticed.

Spiritually gifted individuals love time alone with God. This desire for alone time with God is contrary to our current culture. These perceptive ones may not always be understood by others, but I have noticed through the decades that these gifted ones continue to make decisions with alone time with God being a high priority.

Some of the gifted ones I know ask for help with interpreting now and then. Others like to check in with me daily, at least for a while. They are all learning to function in their gifts, and as they learn, the church and the world around them benefit from their knowledge. Some of them have a double gift of receiving dreams and visions and a gift for interpreting them.

It concerns me that visionaries are sometimes shamed for not interpreting their own dreams. No one can control who will be given certain gifts from God. Those who shame the dreamers for not interpreting all their own dreams may not be able to interpret them either. Understanding is often released from God's hand to those who love.

I mentioned earlier about gifts bumping into each other. For instance, as a person tells of a dream or vision with interpretation, the listener may be given a word of knowledge or a word of wisdom to add to the understanding of the subject. If a sickness is featured in a dream, a gift of healing could rise to correct the problem. God designed the church so that different members would work together in the gifts.

A woman prophesied to me after I had been flowing in this ministry for a few years. She said, "I see you dusting off beautiful

crystal vessels. And I hear the Lord saying, 'She is waking up th
sleeping beauties. I have given my people precious gifts, but many c
them do not know how to use their gifts.'" Her vision described th
ministry I had been moving in every day. Confirmation really can b
an encouragement.

There have been other confirmations that have been significan
in my continued dedication to the service of the King. A few year
ago, when I was eating breakfast in a restaurant before Sunday schoo
I caught a glimpse of something in my spirit. I saw cradles lined u
to my right, and all at once, I saw them tip over, and they deposite
sweet babies into incubators. Knowledge was sealed within me a
I saw this happening. I knew the babies would develop very fast i
these incubators. I knew that these babies were some of the gifte
ones, and I knew that my ministry was like an incubator. Lots c
cradles have tipped over since I saw that vision, and many gifted one
have fallen into my lap.

Although teaching them how to flow in their ministries is m
first concern, Father also shows me their needs as human being
Sometimes, a soul wound or lack of development will hinder one fro
moving forward in the calling. We may work on emotional healing c
forgiveness, just as any Christian mentor would do. I always let ther
decide the degree of help they receive from me. If they only desir
help with their dreams, I help them with their dreams.

When dream interpretation is what they desire, it's mor
business-like in our relationship. We share knowledge and go our ow
ways until they ask for help with another dream. Others need mor
personal ministry. There is no therapy in my ministry; I work on
spiritual level. When the little birds find their wings, they fly away!

It is an honor to work with these gifted ones. God has entruste
me with this task of interpreting dreams, and it never ends. I wi

think I am done for the day, but some of them will take naps, and it starts all over again.

It has been interesting hearing the testimonies. I learned that some love notes are sent to many, while some are sent to a few. Fragrances from heaven are detected much more often than flavors. I learned that if I asked about both, I would almost always hear about fragrances. So, I asked about flavors, and I heard a few testimonies about them, but I heard many more reports about fragrances, even though I did not include them in the question. Likewise, every Christian seems to learn to discern that small, still voice, but only a few tell of hearing the audible voice of God.

I have experienced the fragrance phenomenon twice in my life, more than thirty years apart. Both times, it was totally unexpected. The first fragrance experience was when I was awakened in the middle of the night in a Mexican village on my first mission trip. I could smell flowers that reminded me of a honeysuckle vine. When I was a child, I had enjoyed playing out in my backyard with the fragrance of honeysuckle wafting through the breeze in my direction. But this fragrance was even more special. It was like none other that I have ever experienced before or since.

The next morning, I walked all around the house and yard, looking for the flowers, and there were none. As we began to get acquainted and heard more about our pastoral family, I learned that ten days earlier, the pastor's wife had smelled flowers, but there were no flowers in the house. The pastor heard from the Lord, "When you smell the flowers, you will know that prayers are being prayed for this place. The fragrance of flowers is a symbol for the prayers of the saints."

Smelling the flowers occurred my first night there. The next day, two other mission teams arrived unannounced. All three mission teams had intercessors praying for them. It was summer but not as hot as usual in that area, which was appreciated because the village had no air conditioning. I believe the good weather was a result of all the prayers that were prayed. Also, I believe the prayers were important in helping the three teams to work together. The three teams flowed together as one. The unity was as sweet as the fragrance of the flowers.

It was not unusual for this pastor's house to be immersed in supernatural occurrences. Since they lived in a remote village with no telephone, they received numerous visions that visitors would arrive. The first time my brother traveled to their home, he drove there with a man they called "Brother Bob." The pastor received a vision of Brother Bob driving in a pick-up truck with a man wearing a hat. They drove up to the house in a pick-up, and my brother was wearing a hat, which was no surprise to the pastor's family.

Supernatural occurrences have popped up all through my life. My first vision was about four decades ago, and I have continued to have visions since then, usually when I was least expecting them. When I was six and I heard a children's sermon in vacation Bible school, I had a profound salvation experience. After that, for a few years, I would feel the moving of the Holy Spirit during the Nazarene altar services. I would go down to the altar to kneel and pray with the old people. When I was eleven, I began to be asked to read poems and readings in my church. When I would stand to read, the Holy Spirit would move over the congregation from east to west every time. I would see those tender, Nazarene souls get out their handkerchiefs to dry their eyes. I had no control over what was happening. I just showed up and opened up. I was only a child reading from a script, with no training, but I was a chosen mouthpiece. It was not something I had prayed for and quite a surprise. Later in my life, I was caroling at Christmas time at the nursing home, and an older woman from our church told me, "I remember when you were eleven and twelve years old, and you began to speak in our church." She had tears in her eyes as she talked about this.

In my early twenties, I began to sing in the church. As I would sing solos, I would feel the presence of the Holy Spirit. My face would get warm, and my forehead and lips would burn with the fire of God. I really didn't know how to operate in my gifts, but the Holy Spirit is a teacher. We are trained by the Holy Spirit as we yield to the will of the Heavenly Father. I began to sing new songs to the Lord. My mother said, "I have been hearing about people with a psalmist ministry. I think that's what you are." I knew that David was a psalmist, but that's all I knew about psalmists. I just kept singing spontaneously as the words and melodies came into my heart. I still do.

Getting to know God and attempting to serve Him has been the most exciting and fulfilling part of my life, even to the point of consuming me. After all these years, I am still learning. I have an increasing desire to know my Maker in a greater and more significant way. I desire a deeper revelation of the nature of Almighty God as I draw nearer to His heart.

A couple of years ago, I was dealing with my husband's illness. I was his caretaker as he progressed into the later stages of Alzheimer's before his death. I had other challenges in my life as well.

I asked the Lord to give me a clue about what He had for me in the future. God had communicated with me when I first awakened many times through the years, so I asked Him to show me the first thing in the morning upon awakening. I had expected to wake up with words in my mind, which is what had happened before. But thirty-two years after the flowers in Mexico, I awakened to the smell of blueberry muffins!

One of the most pleasant memories from my youth was waking up to the aroma of blueberry muffins as my mother yelled from the kitchen, "Blueberry muffins! Wake up, kids! We've got blueberry muffins!" The sweet memory of Mama and her blueberry muffins is a blessing to this day.

I believe God's message about my future is that He has sweet surprises waiting for me. The muffins were always a pleasant surprise because I never knew what Mama would be fixing for breakfast, and the muffins were my favorite. (For readers who have not lived in our southern states, I may need to explain that in Texas, we fix a lot of things that are not broken.)

Just as the muffins were sweet surprises scattered through my younger years, I believe that God will scatter sweet things throughout my later years. I am envisioning a scavenger hunt planned by my loving Heavenly Father. As I walk through these trying times, Father will have some sweet things strewn along the way. Although the future is unknown, one thing is certain—God will be there to guide me into each new adventure

Love Notes from Heaven

I have interviewed friends on social media and gained more insight as I heard their stories.

———————•———————

Dar from Florida says,

> I remember several times when a loved one passed
> from this world that I would be praying and thinking
> about them. I would be meditating on God's words
> and promises. Each time, suddenly—I would smell
> roses. It was like assurance from the Lord.

———————•———————

Judy from New Jersey tells of her experiences, "In our House of Prayer, I often smelled incense. In the main meeting room, I often smelled butterscotch. Butterscotch is sweet and pleasant and something God knows I really like."

———————•———————

Carla from Texas said,

> After accepting Christ and receiving full healing
> from Him, I was awakened in the wee hours of the
> morning. I could have sworn He called my name; I
> was carrying much guilt and crying. It felt like God
> poured warm oil over my head down to the tips of
> my toes. I knew I was in the presence of God.

Carla's tactile experience of feeling oil poured over her remind me of the experience I had after the great revival in 1992. As w gathered at the end of the church service to pray for the needs o one another, I leaned over to pray for someone. When I bowed m head in prayer, I felt something warm pour over the back of my necl Nothing in the natural realm had poured out because the back o my neck was not wet. Father had poured out the anointing oil of th Holy Spirit upon me.

That night at church, I prayed for several people, including successful carpenter who had been faithful to support the churc financially. He told me, "I am missing a kneecap after an acciden when playing football with my son. If it keeps on hurting like thi I don't know how I will support my family." Of course, I prayed fo him in faith.

The next time I saw him, he said he was able to work withou pain, and he was even able to lay carpet down on his knees. I was s happy that this man was restored and he could continue to worl supporting his family and his church. He never again spoke of pai or disability.

Did God give the carpenter a new kneecap? I think so. I believe Go gave him the creative miracle he needed. God is faithful to the faithful

I have also seen His mercy poured out on the not so faithfu When people ask me to pray for them, but they have not always don their best, I always advise them to repent and throw themselves o God's mercy. Our God is rich in mercy. After all, God "sendeth rai on the just and on the unjust" (Matthew 5:45).

Father is a bookkeeper who never misses a detail, so we will se a lot of His faithfulness poured out on the faithful. The carpente had been generous with the church beyond his tithe. When h needed a creative miracle, his Creator created one for him. We wer in a remote, little town. There were no big-name healing evangelists around, so the Healer moved through me as I was just learning.

Some of the most interesting testimonies were those who had a taste supernaturally manifest. Since supernatural experiences of flavors are rarer than fragrance experiences, I had to seek more for these testimonies. God does not seem to be as willing to release flavors as readily as He releases fragrances, but He does send them at times. As I was writing this, I remembered being told of flavors appearing while a friend was dieting. When she told me this many years ago, her report was my first time to hear a flavor testimony. When she would get hungry, she would put just a little bit of cottage cheese on the end of a teaspoon, and when she put it in her mouth, she would taste a succession of flavors as they were bursting with flavor in her mouth. She spoke of bell peppers and strawberries and all kinds of things she enjoyed. These little bites of cottage cheese made her feel full and satisfied, and she was able to lose weight without feeling deprived. Another friend did not speak of flavors, but she told me she had been trying to eat moderately but suddenly had a craving; she prayed and suddenly felt very full. This kind of thing does not happen often, but I am also reporting unusual experiences. "O taste and see that the LORD is good: blessed is the man that trusteth in him" (Psalm 34:8).

Linda from England had an unusual taste experience. She says,

> I had been ill with strange symptoms when I put a
> mint in my mouth. I realized that it didn't taste like
> a mint but recognized the taste from my childhood.
> I asked God what it was, and He reminded me that

they were called "Victory V's." I didn't think they still sold them, but the shop had a packet, and the packet said, "Forged in Strength," with a picture of an anvil on a strong arm. God was telling me that I was on the anvil being forged for strength, and we had the victory!

Linda says that God reminds her of this whenever she is going through real times of pressure.

This experience that Linda had reminds me of something that happened to me. My experience was not one of tasting but rather one of seeing. I saw a picture of a cloud that a woman had taken that was positioned over her town.

With my natural eyes, I saw a monster with sharp teeth in the cloud picture. I described what I saw, hoping that my description would encourage intercessors to step up their prayer efforts for the area. I felt that prayer would lessen the grip of this local principality over their town. The woman who took the picture acted like I had lost my mind. Later, I understood why.

When I went back to look at the cloud picture in a couple of days, I saw something very different. I saw only a cluster of fluffy clouds. They looked quite pleasant. The Lord had previously shown me the evil presence that had been wielding some power over the inhabitants of the town. Although it was not manifested in a way that others could see, the Holy Spirit had enabled me to see what was there with my natural eyes. God had shown me what loomed overhead. They need to gain victory over this with prayer. As prayer goes forth for the inhabitants of the earth and the people begin to walk in greater purity, the principalities have some of their power stripped from them.

We do not go directly into the second heaven (up in the sky) with our words in direct combat with these principalities. We do not address them directly nor do we practice spiritual warfare against them up in the sky. Heavenly Father will one day remove these powers from the sky, but for now, they are allowed to live there. However, human beings can exercise great authority over the earth in spiritual warfare as they move in the name of Jesus. God gave Adam authority over the earth, but Adam soon gave it up when he allowed sin to enter the garden. However, as redeemed human beings, we can exercise authority on the earth under the banner of Jesus' name. God moves through believers as they move in faith. As we pray and reach out to the souls around us and they are redeemed, they change, and their environment changes. As this change occurs, the hold of these dark powers is loosened.

Christine from Missouri asked to know the will of God. She did not pray a specific prayer, but she was putting forth a general plea to understand truth. Christine was at a performance that featured "prophetic warfare dance." (I have never observed this type of ministry, but this is Christine's testimony.) One of the members of this ministry team greeted the guests and prayed for God to send healing oil upon Christine. This oil was expressed as a sweet oil, so it must have been mixed with honey. Christine says, "I tasted honey in my mouth during the performance." Then she goes on to say that this happened a month after she was saved. The Lord gave her a confirming sign when she was a brand-new Christian. Christine is an artist who moves in anointing as the Holy Spirit inspires her.

Christine's testimony reminds me of a powerful occurrence in my own devotional life. One day, as I was praying in my house, I had a vision with my natural eyes. Most of my visions have been with my spiritual eyes, but I have had some with my natural eyes.

From up over my head over my right shoulder, I suddenly saw a golden liquid pouring down. It happened quickly, but it was clear as I saw it with my natural eyes. Father spoke to me in my spirit, "You must allow the oil to be mixed with honey, so you can feed my hungry, hungry people!" I did not taste the oil and honey, but I saw it flowing. The Spirit of the Lord has instructed and corrected me since then, and these messages were aligned with the vision and the words delivered with it several years ago.

Elsie from Texas gives a testimony of total surrender as she chased after the presence of

God. The Lord did not disappoint her. "He hath filled the hungry with good things" (Luke

1:53). Elsie says,

> I was so hungry for God—just Him and nothing else. We were leaving a strict, religious community. I was crying out to God as He was stripping me of everything familiar. Everything that was my security for forty-plus years, I was bringing to Him. My hunger for Him became more real than the air that I breathed. I literally tasted the sweetness of His nature every time I thought about what He was doing in my heart. I tasted a beautiful taste in my mouth—when I

talked about what He means to me—when the scales kept coming off my eyes—when the veil was coming off my mind—it was a life-changing chapter in my life. It was a heavenly flavor like a sweetness I can't describe here on earth. It was the same flavor every time. The closest thing to it on this earth would be honey from a real honeycomb. It would come to me in my secret chamber with my bridegroom. The taste would come to me when I would share with others what He was doing in my life—adding to my story.

Elsie goes on to say, "I have another experience. He came to me n a vision. He gave me oil...wine...bread."

------------------------•------------------------

Mindi from Wisconsin says, "I have not tasted, but I have smelled a fragrance. This was a beautiful sweetness, like the fragrance of honey filled the room—hard to describe. I have also smelled the ourning incense."

------------------------•------------------------

Lisa of Colorado tells us, "I could smell my grandmother's perfume in my living room one day. She had passed decades earlier. I was going through a tough time, and I believe I was allowed to smell her perfume to bring peace."

I believe Lisa was right. The fragrance of her grandmother's perfume was certainly not a visit from her grandmother. There is a division between heaven and earth, even though there is a cloud of

witnesses beholding the activities of earth. We are told not to seek
the services of a necromancer (one who attempts to contact spirits
that have passed on). God told Israel not to take on the practices of
the heathen nations around them.

> *When thou art come into the land which the LORD
> thy God giveth thee, thou shalt not learn to do after the
> abominations of those nations. There shall not be found
> among you any one that maketh his son or his daugh-
> ter pass through the fire, or that useth divination, or
> an observer of times, or an enchanter, or a witch. Or a
> charmer, or a consulter with familiar spirits, or a wiz-
> ard, or a necromancer. For all that do these things are
> an abomination to the LORD: and because of these
> abominations the LORD thy God doth drive them out
> before thee. Thou shalt be perfect with the LORD, thy
> God.*

Deuteronomy 18:9–13

Leslie from Florida smelled her dad's cologne a year after his
death, and she was comforted. She heard her name being called and
felt her arm being touched. Leslie had never heard that voice before.
(It was not her father's voice.) Leslie believes that God's voice spoke
to her, and God's hand touched her arm to comfort her. I agree with
her conclusion.

Luke 16:26 speaks of the division between people of the earth
and those who have gone out into eternity, "Between us and you
there is a great gulf fixed: so that they which would pass from hence

to you cannot; neither can they pass to us, that would come from thence."

———————————•———————————

Jenny from Georgia tells of, "One night when I was with a few people in the war room (a room used for prayer and spiritual warfare) at church, the room was suddenly filled with the fragrance of lemons." She goes on to say that there were just a few gathered for that mid-week prayer meeting.

Again, the Lord was faithful to the faithful ones. He met them there with His presence.

They were refreshed with the crisp, fresh fragrance of lemons.

I have heard several reports of lemons.

———————————•———————————

Another report was from Pamela from Georgia, who said,

Once when painting (a spiritual picture) during a
church service, I kept messing up the gold lines I was
painting that represented pages in our own personal
books in heaven,
suddenly I smelled a lemony, citrus scent, and then
God gave a prophetic message and prayer for the
congregation.

I was interested in the message that accompanied the lemon scent. And I hoped she could remember it. Here it is,

God gave me a message about washing the people
as He extended mercy to them. He assured them
that He was forgiving them as they repented. God
was making the pages of their books as white, clean
pages. He told them He was ready to forgive their
mistakes and move on.

She continued, "I had many positive responses to this. When this
message was shared at a women's meeting, a woman gave her life to
Christ after she heard this message repeated."

Another fragrance occurrence happened when I was teaching
special education, but I was not the one who detected it. Students
would leave their own classrooms and come into my classroom for
instruction. A student told me that she always liked to come into my
room. Then she said, "It always smells like cake."

I never smelled the cake, and none of my other students
mentioned it. My conclusion is that the Holy Spirit must have
manifested a sweet fragrance for her every time she walked into my
room. It was meant to be a blessing just for her. Like many of the
supernatural experiences I have had through the years and that I have
heard from others, I do not always know why they happened. My
guess is that they are answers to prayers or by the sovereign will of
God. Those who prayed the prayers may have passed into eternity
years before the supernatural occurrences manifested.

———————•———————

Christine from Maine says,

We were worshipping outside on our front lawn as
I was singing and playing a musical instrument. I

looked up and saw the most beautiful angel wing...
just one...but beautiful. It spoke to my heart. God's
angelic beings are ever-present, guarding over us...
and enjoying our worship of the One and Only
Jesus!!

It was interesting that she only saw one wing. This reminds me
of the scripture, "For we know in part, and we prophesy in part" (1
Corinthians 13:9).

———————•———————

Meadow of Texas testifies that,

While on the porch in 2019, conversing with the
Lord, I saw the heavens open up, and I saw war
horses and armor and swords...there was chaos...I
saw a soldier on a horse being slain by an angel...and
then the heavens shut up. I felt God was showing
me the war and that I should tell people that it was
happening because He was giving me the message
that "the time is now."

Meadow goes on to say, "He is nearer than people know, and He
has the victory. I did not feel fearful at all." Meadow believes that
the return of Jesus is soon, and she says that the Lord continues to
impress this upon her.

———————•———————

Linda from Pennsylvania says,

> This was in 2008. We were having a cookout in our
> front yard. My husband and daughter were outside.
> They were talking, and I was worshipping our Lord,
> looking up in the sky, talking to Jesus. Suddenly, I
> saw the name *Jesus*, and it was breathtaking. Jesus is
> so beautiful.

———————————— • ————————————

Nancy from Alabama tells of what she saw in the sky. She told
the people with her, "Look what I just saw in the sky." Nancy had
been giving spiritual encouragement to a single dad, and when she
looked up, an angel with a shofar in his hands was overhead, and it
looked like the angel was blowing the shofar.

———————————— • ————————————

Also, some of the people spoke of unusual cloud formations.
Many have told me of visions of clouds manifesting into pictures in
the sky.

I have never seen an angel blowing a shofar, even though I have
seen three angels in my lifetime, but I have heard a shofar in prayer
meetings out in a glory barn in western Oklahoma. I heard this
shofar sound on two different evenings, and others did not hear it. I
looked around the room both times to see if someone had brought a
horn, but there was no horn. The low, slow sound of the shofar was
relaxing and peaceful.

Not long after the shofar sounds, I drove my friend, Anita, to a
women's meeting when she was asked to speak. I drove several women

to the meeting, and it was a distance of sixty miles, so we had time to discuss the meeting as I drove them home. This town was known to be rough, with an infestation of sin that had made them notorious since its founding out on the frontier. I was glad she had an opportunity to minister in this town, as I was hoping for a breakthrough for this area.

As Anita spoke, I saw a storm manifest, and I heard it, as well. I could hear the storm brewing overhead. I saw it get dark outside the windows. There was a lot happening with speakers and a little girls' dance team. It was wonderful. Then, it seemed like the storm came into the building with us as darkness invaded the room. There seemed to be a real note of victory as the meeting came to an end. Something broke, and we all felt that the meeting was a success.

As I was driving home, we talked about the meeting. I said, "It got good after we got through that storm. I'm glad I do not have to drive in it." I told what I had seen and heard. After a brief moment of silence, they all chimed in with, "Cynthia, there was no storm...you must have sensed that in the Spirit."

Oh my! I certainly did! It's amazing how many firsts we experience in the Spirit. We are learning as we are serving. I had seen and heard the storm with my natural eyes and ears, and I had felt an eeriness within. Sometimes, we seek to discern matters, and other times, discernment rises suddenly within.

On two different occasions, I have seen angels clearly with my natural eyes. In the middle of the night, I suddenly awakened and opened my eyes. I saw my late husband's guardian standing watch while he was sleeping. I believe the angel knew I saw him, but he never took his eyes off my husband. He was a faithful guardian. The angel was tall and large, and he looked like a man from antiquity with his medium brown hair in a bowl cut, wearing a tunic of mingled blue and green. My husband was older than me, so this angel had guarded him for a long time. Since then, I have heard that angels begin to take on some of the characteristics of the humans they guard. His hair was the color of my husband's hair when he was young, and until I married my husband late in his life, he wore blue and green shirts most of the time.

His angel was faithful to the end. A few years before my husband's death, he was carrying two casserole dishes, one stacked on top of the other, and he fell in front of our church after a potluck dinner. His hands were full, and he could not break his fall but fell back on the sidewalk. The outcome could have been terrible, but he did not have a scratch or bruise, did not have any pain, and was not hurt in any way. I believe his guardian angel helped him on the way down. I was grateful, but obviously, the angel's duties were confined to his human; protecting my prized pottery was not his concern, and pottery could be replaced.

Several years back, when I was taking the census, I had to drive to counties far from my home, traveling to remote areas in the country and into some bad neighborhoods in the towns. I was trying to be careful. The Lord was faithful to take care of me. To simplify matters, I kept returning to the same gas station where the attendant would put gas in my car, saving me the trouble. The gas station was small, and I was almost always the only customer. The attendant was always friendly. I had always pulled in so that my driver's door was toward the highway, but I pulled in differently that day, so the driver's door was against the door to the gas station. As usual, I was the only customer. If I had needed to have escaped, it would have been impossible.

Suddenly, I looked up and saw two men who looked like each other. There was no car, but they just suddenly appeared. I was watching and paying attention as they seemed to be talking to each other a little bit. I was watching and wondering about the twins who just popped up in the gas station driveway just a few feet away. They were average in every way with a clean-cut appearance—average height and weight, with medium brown hair. Their hair was the same color as my husband's guardian angel, but the similarity ended there. My husband's angel had been focused on one activity—standing guard over him and never taking his eyes off his human. The twins seemed to be checking out their environment as they talked among themselves. I now believe they were discussing possible strategies. These medium men had a quality of being able to blend in nicely, and I think the blending in was a part of their assignment.

To my surprise, they were suddenly behind my car! Although I was paying attention, I did not see them walk to the back of my car. It would have been impossible not to see them on the driver's side since I was parked so closely, and I had been watching the passenger side. They appeared in my rearview mirror as quickly as they had appeared before me.

At that time, I obviously had not processed all of this in my mind, but as I was driving away, the Holy Spirit spoke to me, "Do not go back there again." The message was clear. I still have questions that may not be answered until I go out into eternity—questions such as: "Why did God send two average angels instead of a big one? Do the twins guard me all the time, or were they sent in for a special mission? Will I ever see them again in this life?"

In retrospect, as I think about them, they did seem to be average in every way except one. These men looked very pure. Thinking back over the situation, it would be hard to imagine that either one of them had ever sinned. As I remember the countenances of these men and the circumstances of their arrival into my life, I must conclude that they are God's holy angels.

Maggie from Arizona saw something unusual as she was driving her car. She was asking God to help her with her finances when her attention was drawn to her car radio. The radio was turned off, and there was no sound. Maggie took a photograph of the unusual phenomenon with her phone, and she sent the picture to me. Her photo showed a clear picture of the word "*money*" on her radio in all capital letters. This word stayed written on her radio for eighty miles as the sound of static was heard over the radio.

Elizabeth from Connecticut told of a vision she saw when she was fourteen or fifteen years old. She remembers it well in her golden years. According to Elizabeth,

> I am now seventy-seven, and I had a vision of Jesus as a young teen. This was just after my friend had died of leukemia.
> I would go to bed at night and talk to God and cry myself to sleep. But one night, I went to bed and started thinking of this friend and started talking to God. I remember my prayer was always for God to take me to be with Jesus. I fell asleep again but woke up in the middle of the night, and there, by the foot of my bed, was Jesus.
> It was dark, and I saw that Jesus had a long, white robe. His hair was long. I heard Him say that my friend was with Him in heaven. I cannot remember how He left. I just went back to sleep.
> I never cried again, but more than that, I was never

36

fearful again. Not that night or ever again, not fearful about anything. Now I know that He can still come to us, or He can send angels if need be. What a treat that I was able to get to see Jesus at fourteen or fifteen years old. What a wonderful Father we have.

Elizabeth has basked in the memory of this one supernatural event throughout her entire life, but

———————— • ————————

Kaye from Texas reports that she has had a lot of supernatural experiences:

The first one was when God was introducing me to the spiritual side of things. My husband and I were walking together in Corinth, Texas, in 2016. I told my husband to look up to see the plumbline in the sky. We went to the church service that night, and Chuck Pierce said, "God has put a plumbline in the sky." God usually confirms what I see.

Kaye tells of another experience, "I was on my way to a Trump rally, and I saw a train up in the sky. I heard 'Get on the Trump train.' Then everyone around me started saying to get up on the Trump train."

———————— • ————————

Linda from Maryland says,

I had a vision God showed me while I was being operated on. (This was when she was under

37

anesthetic, but God was still able to communicate with her spirit, and she remembered it.) I saw faceless people in the background, behind the glass encasement, and they were waving at me to keep going because I was told I would die in a short time if I didn't have the operation. I know that was God's way of telling me He was with me all the way.

I believe the faceless beings were angels sent to encourage her, and most likely, there were unseen angels helping with this serious surgery.

———————————•———————————

Barbara from Wales said that she was living in northern England when she came to know the Lord after attending a Billy Graham meeting:

Minister and his wife took me under their wings, and they wanted me to travel to North Wales for a weekend conference. This is where I had a wonderful vision of Jesus while two hundred people were praising the Lord. Jesus came towards me. He was wearing a long, brown robe with a white rope around it. He smiled, put out His hand, and said, "I have found you." At that moment, gold liquid poured out all over me...it was the most beautiful thing that happened to me. I was full of peace.

———————————•———————————

Mary from Texas tells of seeing a shell in a vision:

Yesterday, I saw a big, beautiful shell. It was colored red on the outside. On the inside was a clock with black numbers. It was ten minutes until 2:00. I sense that red means redemption. The almost two o'clock is double portion—double for your trouble. It's about the double portion beginning to flow. The shell perhaps means protection of life, and the shell is a symbol of birth, good fortune, and resurrection.

I agree.

Regena from Oregon experienced a beefy taste in her mouth:

I had a taste of roast beef as the Lord spoke to me about Himself. At first, I wondered if I might be crazy, but I know now that this was from the Holy Spirit. He was speaking to me about having a beefy hunger for the beefy things of God's Word and of His Spirit.

Petra relates to us about her dream,

I had a dream where a lady I knew held a prophetic women's retreat (which actually happened, but I could not attend). In the dream, she sent me anointing oil by post (by mail). When I opened it to smell it, it touched my lips, and there was a minty taste in my mouth. Since then, I have associated mint with the prophetic.

Petra's dream of having something imparted to her in a dream even though she was not able to attend the retreat, reminds me of something that happened to me. God knows who is hungry to learn more from Him and those who desire to lean in closer. The men in our church were able to attend a men's retreat which featured a gifted Bible teacher. I was happy for them to go, but I wished I could hear the teaching, too. When the men were away at the retreat, I spent some quality time with God in my house. One evening, I went to my keyboard and began to sing and pour out my heart to the Lord. When I sang one song, "Behold, I Stand at the Door and Knock," about Jesus knocking at the door to my heart and His fellowship when we allowed Him in, I felt a very strong presence of the Lord. The Holy Spirit was all over me and moving within me. After the men came back, they told of their wonderful retreat, with its main theme being "Behold, I Stand at the Door and Knock." God has many ways to feed those who hunger and thirst for His presence.

Sarah from England witnesses a new dimension being added to her fellowship with the Lord one morning. She had gone to bed the night before, telling Jesus how much she loved spending time with Him and how satisfying His presence was to her. She jokingly told Him, "I would like to have a full English breakfast with You in the morning." When she awakened, the aroma of a full English breakfast filled the house. Sarah really enjoyed her fellowship with Jesus that morning. Did she look around the house for a logical

40

explanation? It seems that we always do this! Of course, no natural phenomenon was present; this was one more supernatural event in the life of a Christian who treasured the Lord's presence.

Marcela from Mexico tells of this:

> While in worship at my church, I smelled something like a sweet vanilla cake. It was quite strong, but none of the others could smell it. I asked if anyone was baking a cake, but there was no cake. I think the meaning of this is about the sweet revelation of the Word of God ministering in my life.

I have spent a lot of time with Amy in the inbox of my phone in the last few years, with almost daily contact. I have enjoyed getting to know her as a person, hearing of her struggles and triumphs. Since the flavors are rare, I thought I should ask Amy because of her spiritual sensitivity. Communicating with His Covenant children via flavors is one more love note that God has for His own—well, some of His own do experience this.

Amy made this observation: "It always happened when I was riding in the car when my husband was driving." I have wondered if she felt free while she was riding in the car, not responsible for what was happening as her husband drove. Her mind was not hindered by distractions.

Amy continued, "One day, when he was driving, the taste of cotton candy came into my mouth. I have always liked cotton candy, and I loved it as a child." So, it seems that Heavenly Father just wanted to give her a sweet tweak on these days she tasted the cotton candy. As with some of the other testimonies, I could not find any deeper meaning, even after questioning. Our precious Lord is a God of blessing as He reaches out to us and as He builds relationships with each one of us.

God is a master of details, and He remembers every detail of our likes and dislikes. Even as I kept a baby book and recorded the details of my daughter's early activities and favorite things, Heavenly Father keeps records of His dear children, and He likes to share things with them to bring them joy. Father is also faithful as we repent—to blot out every sin with the perfect blood of His only begotten Son as He continues to keep adding to our books.

> *Then they that feared the LORD spake often one to another: and the LORD hearkened, and heard it, and a book of remembrance was written before him for them that feared the LORD, and that thought upon his name.*

Malachi 3:16

I asked Amy to tell us about other flavors, and this was her answer:

> There have been a few times getting the taste of Mexican food and barbecue—again in the car. One occasion was during a trip to Texas when we still lived up north. We came back for a visit, and my husband had submitted a request for a transfer to the Dallas area. (Amy is from the Dallas/Fort Worth

area and wanted to return.) I don't think the transfer has gone through yet. Mexican food and barbecue are Texas flavors. That was confirmation that the job transfer to Texas would go through.

I agree completely. God gave her confirmation with two recurring Texas flavors. They are now nicely situated in her home state.

Those who have flavors suddenly manifest do seem to be given a little taste of heaven, especially when they experience delightful tastes they have not experienced on earth. One day, as Amy's husband was driving her through Detroit, she suddenly had a taste of hell. This is what she told me, "When you leave Metro Detroit, the atmosphere shifts. Landing in Detroit at the airport is like landing in a very heavy oppression—like a thick fog." (Amy is spiritually gifted and senses things in the spirit realm that others would miss.)

I have heard reports that God has shown ministers that there will be a great revival in Detroit. I am glad to know this, especially after hearing from Amy. There are many other American cities that desperately need revival, as well.

Amy continues, "I suddenly smelled sulfur, and I tasted it in my mouth. I believe God allowed me to experience this because I am an intercessor, and He wanted me to pray for the city."

———— · ————

Vickie from Florida says that God speaks to her through nature. Just when she needed to see a sign from God, she looked up and saw a rainbow in the sky. She was comforted after her father's death when she looked up and saw the rainbow.

On another occasion, Vickie was having serious spiritual struggles. She felt the oppression of evil settling over her. She prayed and did some fasting, but she felt no release. Christian friends came to her with words of assurance, but she was unable to break through into victory. This travail of her soul lasted about three months. She had lost seventy pounds, unintentionally, in this three-month time frame.

She even woke up one night with an evil presence pressing down over her as if holding her hostage. Vickie had left the Lord's side for a time, but she had returned, and she was calling out to Him for help. She wanted to be reassured that God had accepted her back; she wanted to return to the fellowship she had once had with her Savior.

Even though she had returned to the Lord, even though she had repented, she did not feel the assurance she desired. Vickie told me that she understood the people in the Old Testament who rent (tore) their clothes and sat in sackcloth and ashes. So great was her agony.

Vickie had allowed fear to move into her mind in such a way that the fear was blocking the words of assurance. She was not able to feel God's presence, nor was she hearing His voice. One day, she did hear Father say, "Come home, daughter. Come home, now." But even so, it was hard for her to break through those barriers of fear to receive what she needed.

One day, she saw a rainbow, and as her husband was driving to the grocery store, she asked the Lord, "If there is hope for me, please let me see another rainbow." In the fifteen-minute drive, she saw seven or eight rainbows. Everywhere she looked, there was another rainbow. She is still amazed at the number of rainbows she saw that day during that short drive.

Vickie regained her faith, and she now testifies to God's greatness. Our God of signs and wonders releases them upon mankind to achieve His purposes on the earth. The signs that Father released as rainbows brought Vickie back into fellowship with Him. "I do et my bow in the cloud, and it shall be for a token of a covenant between me and the earth" (Genesis 9:13).

When I heard Vickie's story, I remembered the song, "Tie a Yellow Ribbon Round the Old Oak Tree." In the song, the man wonders if he will be welcomed back home, so he writes a letter telling his family to tie a yellow ribbon around the old oak tree if he is welcome. Otherwise, he would stay on the bus and start his life over again, alone. The tree was covered in many yellow ribbons, meaning that all was forgiven, and he was loved.

In Vickie's life, there were many rainbows attesting to the generous nature of our God. Heavenly Father had placed them all over the sky, everywhere she turned. In His extravagant love, He had made sure that His message was clear. Vickie came home to Father's arms that day, and she has remained.

As I have collected testimonies for this book, I have noticed reoccurring patterns showing some of the reasons for God's communicating with His Covenant children. So many of these love notes were sent to comfort and assure the Covenanters of His acceptance and warmth.

In the patterns, I have noticed degrees of intimacy in these love notes. In Elsie's life, there was a passionate love for the Lord, and He did not send her away empty-handed. Father met her at the point of her zeal for His presence.

This morning, this scenario came into my mind as I was walking through my house, and I believe it was from the Lord:

A young man sees a lovely young woman. I will call them Bill and Betty. Bill is interested in Betty and would like to date her, but Betty tells him she just wants to be friends. Being a gentleman, Bill agrees to her terms of friendship. After all, Bill values her friendship and hopes she will grow fonder of him in time. Bill thinks Betty would be a good wife if things develop as he hopes. As time goes on, Bill and Betty continue their friendship, but it is a bit one-sided. When Betty has car problems, she calls Bill, and he goes over to help. Betty always says, "Thank you," and she is never rude, but she is never warm, and Bill respects her boundaries.

Later, Bill sees Mary, who has many noble qualities he can respect. When he asks her out, she smiles warmly and accepts. The anticipation of going out the first time is mutual. Mary dresses up and sprays on perfume. Mary allows him to open the car door for her, and she enjoys sitting beside him as he drives her to some special place. As the relationship progresses, he asks for her hand in marriage, and they take the holy vows of matrimony for a lifetime together.

I was surprised when this story unfolded as I was walking through my house one morning when I was beginning to write this book. The Lord seeks a warm and loving relationship with all His humans, but there are different levels of receptiveness. Some will accept the Savior to forgive their sins and give Him an hour in the sanctuary on Sunday morning. It's more like a business relationship than a love relationship. The Lord hopes for more warmth in the future as He moves in to help when He hears cries of distress. An important part of this relationship is our consent for Him to move into the inner chambers of our hearts.

In 1992, after a great revival that was a pivot point in my life, the Lord spoke to me one day, "I have no desire for a bride with no passion." I had not been seeking the Lord about anything like this. It seemed to come out of nowhere! But I knew it was from the Lord.

God moved in such a mighty way. That one-week revival in January was followed by three more revival meetings within driving distance in the same year with the same evangelist. The Spirit of the Lord moved upon me all though that year in ways I had not expected. The Holy Spirit began to reveal some of His plans for me.

One day, the Lord said, "I have given you the gift of mercy." I was not sure I had heard correctly. I thought mercy sounded like a fruit of the Spirit, but I found it in Romans, chapter 12, and it is a gift. Many Bible teachers classify the Romans' twelve gifts as "motivational gifts" since they do motivate us to serve the Lord in specific ways, according to our gifting.

We are born with our motivational gifts, and our dominant, motivational gift should be driving a lot of our actions. God puts them there to motivate us to do the things He created us to do. Placing them within us was meant to simplify things. But we can spend time not so close to the Lord, even far away at times, and our hearts can become hardened. Hardened hearts can become confused hearts, causing us not to be motivated according to Father's plans for us.

Sometimes, we become forced into roles we were not created for because of the expectations of others or because of circumstances that try to stuff us into molds where we do not fit.

It took a great move of the Holy Spirit to bring this dominant, motivational gift out of dormancy. When dominant goes dormant, there is a problem. This gift of mercy had surfaced from time to time through the years, but after the revival, the Holy Spirit began to teach me about it, and this teaching continued in various ways.

When God began to talk to me about it, I knew He was also asking my permission to allow Him to move through me in this gift. I knew if I did not agree with His request, He would allow me to do as I wished, but I also knew I would be saying no to Almighty God.

I knew that when I gave God permission to move through me in this gift of mercy, I would be different than before. There would be no turning back. I knew that my personality would take on some changes. It was scary, but I knew that I was working with the Ancient of Days, great in wisdom and love. I had just been mightily touched by His Spirit, and I knew I wanted Him to stay nearby. I consented to God moving through my life however he wished.

Of all the decisions I have made in my life, this has been one of the most important. If I had chosen differently, I would not be the same person I am today, and I like myself better now than before. I realize now that as I had starved this gift and squashed it into submission to my will, I had also starved a major part of my soul.

Heavenly Father, like Bill in the story I previously told, is such a gentleman. He will not violate our free will. Father created us to be free, and we will make our own choices as long as we have breath. Those who inherit a place in the New Jerusalem will be eternally free.

I chose to allow God to move through me as He created me to be, aligned with His plans for me before I was born into the world. I have discovered who I really am, and my true self is easier for me to live with than to try to live according to the expectations of others with different motivating factors. God rescued me from living by scripts He had not written for me, even though it has taken years for me to learn to decode the script with more accuracy. Thank You, Father. Truly, I thank You.

In 1992, as I was walking through my dining room, Jesus spoke to me suddenly, through the Holy Spirit, "You will be *so* glad to see me when I return!" That was all He said, but He said it strongly. This may not seem like a love note to some, but it was. He told me at a time when I was able to receive it, and this has been a help to me, especially as I have seen society become more chaotic and the world condition is less secure. I know that God is watching over His Covenant children as we live through these times.

When Jesus told me this, I knew that He meant that the world would be filled with so many struggles, and we would look up and be so happy to see Jesus in the clouds—our Rescuer, our Savior, the Hero who will come to snatch us out of the clutches of the evil world system gone out of control. Even if the Lord tarries and I pass on into eternity through natural means, those who remain will have the hope of His return.

That was quite a year—1992! My mother told me we were going to have a revival in January. January! I have never heard of a revival in January—not before and not since. Our coldest months are in January and February, and our road crews are not as active as those up north. My mother opened the church she pastored for four revivals every year. I knew people would be driving in from the counties up north, and I worried about their safety on bad roads or with high winds blowing snow, making visibility impossible.

I asked Mama why she would schedule a revival for the last week of January. She told me it was the only time she could get this good evangelist. Then she said, "And the weather may be good. Have you ever thought about that?!" Her soprano voice went up on the last word, and it must have shattered opposition in the spirit realm. The revival was on. In all my life, I have not seen such lovely weather in that area in the last week of January. She was obviously in a huddle with the Father, Son, and Holy Spirit, and they were planning a launch in the Spirit that I have never forgotten.

Mama was right about one thing—he was a good evangelist. That week was a date with destiny, marked on God's calendar. As I was sitting on the pew, I would feel waves of the Holy Spirit moving over me and through me. Wherever I sat, God found me. Sometimes, there was intense heat. I knew that I was in something bigger than I could manage, and I knew that God was sending a lot of His power into our little church. It was as though Father had turned His face toward us, and His eyes were focused upon us. It was not a time to get things wrong.

I came in one Thursday night after I had taught a history class at the community college, and I was ready to pick up my teenage daughter to drive her home. I came in expecting to leave soon with my daughter, so I was in escape mode. My mind was on the thirteen-mile drive home. A quick amen was what I was looking for.

That service did not end until 12:30 a.m., after midnight. The Holy Spirit had work to do, and He was not in a hurry. When the Holy Spirit moved that night, I found I was no longer tired.

I usually tried to avoid meetings at night because of problems sleeping, but after these meetings, I would go home and soon be in lullaby land. I told my mother that I knew it was a true move of God because I could sleep every night after being out late. This was a sign and wonder to me.

The Holy Spirit was introducing me to a new reality—one aligned with the kingdom of God. I remember that the Holy Spirit stayed on me in a powerful way until I got to the bridge that was halfway home. This was about seven miles of driving under the power. Fortunately, this did not affect my driving. My mind was focused on my driving, but the Spirit did not lift. There are so many firsts in this earth's journey with God. During the seven-mile power drive, I wondered if this condition might be permanent until I went out into eternity.

A short time after this, as I was reading the newspaper in my house, the Holy Spirit came upon me in a powerful way. As I said, there are a lot of firsts. I would know now to put the paper down to receive all God would have for me in His chosen moment for an encounter. But I just kept on reading the paper, as the Spirit was manifesting, and I was wondering what would happen next. Oh my. God is patient with His humans. Sometimes, I wonder what God thinks about us as we are learning.

In addition to a total of four revival meetings with the same evangelist within driving distance in the year, my mother also brought in some singing evangelists for other revivals in our local church. I remember 1992 as "the year of revival." As a history teacher, I have studied the golden ages of great civilizations. That was our "Golden Age of Revival."

When there were no guest evangelists in the church, I was taking steps further into my own ministry. My psalmist ministry, which has flourished in some seasons more than others, was moving ahead during that time.

The last of the four revivals in 1992 was in the fall, and it was in a building across the street from my house. It was in the gymnasium of the school I had attended before it had closed and consolidated with the school in the county seat. I looked across the street. The green leaves had just set on the trees I had played under since I was quite young. As I admired the new, green leaves, God spoke to me, "I will move mightily by My Spirit in this town before these leaves fall from the trees." I thought of this promise often as I moved through the summer and into the autumn. As autumn progressed, the trees held tenaciously to the golden leaves. They seemed to stay attached longer than usual, but maybe it just seemed so as I was watching closely with the promise nestled snugly in my heart.

There were three churches in my hometown, this tiny town of only a hundred residents. There was a small denominational church, a slightly larger denominational church that I grew up in, and the church building (the former high school gymnasium) which specialized in camp meetings and revival meetings. My home church had scheduled its revival very close to the time of the revival church and God moved mightily in both revivals. I know because I was in both revivals. Then the golden leaves promptly fell from the trees.

As I was writing this, I remembered the other little church that was just behind our house. Not long after this, they began to bring in a Bible teacher from time to time, and the cars would crowd their parking lot as they opened their Bibles together. God moved upon the entire town.

My hometown was once a prosperous farming community with bustling businesses. Like so many small towns in the area, it has dwindled in size and strength. Yet, God does not forget living, breathing souls, no matter their circumstances. A few years after the great revival, when I had fasted three days and was driving through town, I thought to myself, *This has become a shabby, little town.*

Just then, as I was about to drive by one of the dusty roads that intersected the paved, farm-to-market road, the Holy Spirit spoke suddenly and unexpectedly, "It won't seem so shabby when the glory rolls!" I looked to the right down that dusty road, and there was a big, orange-red ball of fire. It was so real, like I was seeing it with my natural eyes. This is a promise that has not yet been fulfilled, but I know God spoke and showed me the glory that was poised and set to roll. Nothing is too hard for our God.

I have often thought about the "Golden Year of Revival." During that year, I traveled the farm-to-market road into the county seat often because the businesses had closed in my town. I was so immersed in the Spirit; I was not able to travel that thirteen-mile road without praying for every family along the way. When I would see a house or mailbox on that lonely stretch of road, I would pray for them. Sometimes, I would take the alternate route and pray for other families. Later, I learned about a family with serious problems who had worked them out in the time I was praying for them. Only God knows all the good that came from the prayers.

One day as I was driving the path of my prayer pilgrimage, an unknown driver in a pick-up truck passed me, and I was inspired to pray. I followed behind him with my fingertips extended on my steering wheel. As I prayed, I felt a great surge of electricity flowing through my arms and hands. I have wondered what it felt like in his vehicle because I know what was happening in mine. With the launching of this prayer being so powerful, I know the landing must have been effective, whether he felt anything or not.

It was good that I had this time to be drawn close to the Lord. I was attending my mother's church, a non-denominational church, where she was pastoring. She had always carried a heavy prayer load for her church. In the last years of Mama's life, when she was dealing with health issues, the Lord took that prayer load off her. One day, not long before her death, she said that she still prayed in those last years of her life, but God had lifted the heavy load. As the prayer load was taken off her, it was placed on my shoulders. Hearing her tell of this explained a lot to me. I am glad I had experienced the great revival, so I was able to help my mother a bit later when she needed me. After carrying her prayer load for a time, I had a great appreciation for her ministry, and prayer was only a part of the responsibility and anointing she carried.

As I prayed for our local church, I began to have more visions for the church, both local and global. One day as I was praying in my living room, God showed me a crossbow. He impressed upon me the advantage of the local churches working together. A crossbow is harder to pull back to shoot the arrow, but once the arrow is released from the crossbow, it can be launched to a great distance. A simple bow and arrow (a church working independently but not in unity with other churches in some projects and joint revival meetings) could be effective. However, as churches of like faith work together, they have more power. This was especially true in our area because our towns were small, and our churches were small. I think a mega-church would not have this great need. This was a vision about our local area.

Mama would drive me into town as we taught night classes next door to each other in the extension program for the community college. She drove slowly so we would have more time together as we visited and prayed in the car. Mama would flow in ministry as she told me what she had learned through the years about serving God and serving others. I knew that these car trips were my Bible college and spiritual training program. She flowed so naturally in this, even though she was moving in supernatural ministry. I felt she did not realize the significance of her stream of consciousness training because it did flow so naturally, and I still believe this. I knew, but I did not tell her. Her words flowed like a river—a river of life.

As I worked with Mama in ministry, I was amazed at some of the visions the Holy Spirit opened to me. Sometimes, I was a watchman on the wall, and I would warn of dangers approaching. Of all the ministries I have moved in, I would not call this my favorite. I like to teach and counsel more than I like to warn or do deliverance, but I serve as the Spirit moves on me. Mama had to adjust to my warnings because they were alarming, and most of us prefer peace and calm to a watchman on the wall crying out the warning. One day, she told me that God told her that He had posted a watchman at the end of the road; she saw me in a vision as God spoke to her. She understood my warnings after that.

I have received some memorable visions of the church with my spiritual eyes. They were so vivid and made such a great impression upon me; I don't know how they could have made a greater impression if they had been received with my natural eyes. My first vision at age twenty-eight was received with spiritual eyes, and it was about the church.

My first vision was received after I had listened to a Bible teaching at the church, with the main text being from 1 Corinthians 12:27, "Now ye are the body of Christ, and members in particular." As I walked into my house, I immediately caught the vision in my spirit. I saw a blob of flesh rolling down a hill. Then, I saw the flesh take on the arms and legs, hands and feet, fingers and toes. The flesh took on the form of the human body. The vision that came so abruptly was the illustration of the scripture that had been taught earlier.

A small group would gather to pray at our church on Saturday mornings. I have noticed that the prayer meetings in a church tend to be small, but they can be so special. I learned to enjoy these exclusive gatherings of hungry souls. One Saturday, as we prayed, I suddenly caught sight of an old-fashioned treasure chest as I had seen in movies about ocean voyages and pirates. The treasure chest was brimming with jewels as the top was open and held back on its hinges. Jewels had spilled out on the floor around the chest. Many strands of pearls draped over the sides of the treasure chest. It was old but full of valuables, and it was magnificent!

The Lord made me understand that this ancient treasure chest was a symbol of the very mature Christians who were loaded to overflowing with spiritual riches. I have known some of these treasure chests, and I have drawn from their overflowing resources.

The Lord is faithful. I prayed for one tiny church, and God gave me visions of the church universal. We cannot outgive God.

During the next Saturday meeting, God gave me two follow-up visions as we prayed. After we had prayed for a while, I saw a sleek, trim, modern-looking box without a lid. There were brightly colored gemstones filled to the top and heaped up a bit. There were no jewels spilled out on the floor, and there were no strands of pearls draped over the sides.

I understood that this was a younger Christian, one who was faithful and properly developed for their own stage of life. After we had prayed more, I saw a precious, tiny treasure chest. It looked just like the sleek box in the second vision, but it was smaller. The jewels were sparkling just as brightly as the jewels in the bigger boxes, but this third box was tiny. Of course, this little box represented a baby Christian or even a small child who carries the treasure of salvation in his heart. I believe it also represents those who have been taught to honor the Lord, and they honor Him according to their limited understanding, but they have not yet come to the age of accountability to receive Him fully as Savior.

I wonder if I am properly communicating the fullness of the understanding I received concerning the tiny jewel box. I was made to understand how dearly beloved are the newborn baby Christians and how cherished are the little children! Father loves us at all levels of our development.

At this point, I am feeling led to remind the church that we all carry the same glory but in different sizes of containers. The seasoned, mature Christians can pray long, and some of them can sit through long, detailed teachings if they have some intellectual leanings.

Younger Christians are precious glory carriers, but their containers cannot take in as much at one time. Their attention spans are more limited. Heavenly Father is patient with them, and we must be patient. They require frequent, small feedings with some delightful bites strategically placed. They do love their Savior, and sometimes it may even seem that He loves them best! And yet, I know how Father depends on mature Christians.

One Saturday, as I prayed with the prayer team, I felt led to pray about an unnamed business that had moved into a brick building in our county seat. As I began to pray about God removing this from the town, I suddenly exclaimed, "Lord, I ask you to take that building apart, brick by brick!" A year or so after that, a truck pulling a wagon drove into town. They loaded all the bricks on the wagon and carried them away. Thirty years later, almost everyone has forgotten it was ever there. God erased it from the landscape.

From time to time, I continued to have visions about the church in my house. I woke up from a Sunday afternoon nap on my couch. When I opened my eyes and sat up, I saw shadow people as warriors on the battlefield. They were throwing spears, and they never tired of hurling the spears. They threw one after another without stopping. I knew this was the glorious church that would arise at the end of the Church Age, just before Jesus returned. Oh, what a glorious church it will be! "That he might present it to himself a glorious church, not having spot, or wrinkle, or any such thing; but that it should be holy and without blemish" (Ephesians 5:27).

The glorious church will have mighty warriors. Maybe I saw the frontline warriors; they were so impressive. I think there may have been others in supporting roles that I did not see. From what I have seen, I believe healing will come into the church in a greater way because I have seen a healthy, energetic church.

The early church was a powerful force, and I believe the glorious church will be, as well. The early church turned the world upside down. The glorious church will show Christianity at its finest. I truly believe that God has saved the best wine for the last (John 2:10).

I do not predict a year, but I believe it is not far away.

And he said unto them, it is not for you to know the times or the seasons, which the Father hath put in his power. But ye shall receive power, after that the Holy Ghost is come upon you: and ye shall be witnesses unto me both in Jerusalem, and in all Judaea, and in Samaria, and unto the uttermost part of the earth.

Acts 1:7–8

Powerful witnesses will fight their way in through enemy lines with Scripture and spiritual warfare. They will declare the power of the perfect sacrifice and move in faith. "For the weapons of our warfare are not carnal, but mighty..." (2 Corinthians 10:4).

I also saw great strength in the following vision. I saw a stallion reared up on its back legs, and it was the strongest animal I had ever seen in my life. I grew up spending a lot of time on farms and ranches, but I have never seen a horse that strong. It was a black stallion, and I am reminded that if you mix every color of paint together, you wind up with black, so I think the black stallion represents all nations and races in the church. He was powerful and confident.

In recent years, the church has struggled, and some have fallen away, leaving the fellowship. Many Christians have been sick and frail. However, the stallion that suddenly appeared in my living room that day was vibrant and strong. I told my mother that I thought there would be a great change in the end-time church, and I felt the church would walk in health at the end of the age. I still believe this.

I know that many of you identify the church as a female entity because we will eventually live in the New Jerusalem with Old Testament believers, and collectively, we will make up the bride of Christ. In fact, this city itself is called a bride. Not only the church but all true, resurrected believers since time began will be a part o the bride. "And I John saw the holy city, new Jerusalem, coming down from God out of heaven, prepared as a bride adorned for her husband. And the Spirit and the bride say, Come" (Revelation 21:2, 22:17).

The church will be a part of the bride, but it is now functioning as the body of Christ on this earth, and the Lord has always given me visions portraying the body of Christ, the church, as a male entity. "For as the body is one, and hath many members, and all the members of that one body, being many, are one body: so also is Christ" (1 Corinthians 12:12).

When 2 Thessalonians 2:7–8 speaks of the church, "he" is written:

> *For the mystery of iniquity doth already work: only he who now letteth will let, until he be taken out of the way. And then shall that Wicked be revealed, whom the Lord shall consume with the spirit of his mouth, and shall destroy with the brightness of his coming.*

2 Thessalonians 2:7–8

This speaks of the church being taken from the earth, and then the anti-Christ will be revealed.

When I hear Christians speak of the church with a feminine pronoun, I do understand why. When we join other believers in heaven, we will have a name change. We will no longer be known as the body of Christ, but we will be known as the bride of Christ for eternity. With the marriage, there will be a name change. All this to explain why the Lord has given me the visions of the church as the body of Christ. I do realize that Christians tell of God speaking to them about the bride being purified for the bridegroom.

After the visions the Lord has given me about the church, I have not been discouraged when I have heard criticism of the weakness and ineffectiveness of the present-day church. I know the remnant church shall wax valiant. I find it impossible to believe otherwise. God has always worked through a remnant of faithful ones, and He shall do so again. The church shall arise.

When we talk about supernatural experiences, some may get the idea that when we live with one ear open to the Spirit, we are spared the details of this natural world, but this is not so. None of us who have shared testimonies in this book have lived a cloistered life away from the struggles of reality. Some of the most precious times of my life were spent in a little white frame house, just a hop, skip, and a jump from Mama's house. I have not spent my life in an isolated, spiritual retreat, but I did have some sweet times when I would fast breakfast and lunch and spend the day with the Lord when my family was out of the house. I would pray and worship as I did laundry and took care of other chores around the house. When I was teaching school and had a long drive to work, I learned to pray in the car. I have lived an ordinary life, but I have had an extraordinary life in the Spirit, which has accelerated in certain seasons.

Since the Lord is such a gentleman, considering my frame, I have gotten to experience many lovely things with God's filter preventing me from seeing ugly things that were not able to

get through to my consciousness. I do not know what the Lord will allow me to see in the future, but I trust Him.

Even when I have reached out in mercy to deliver those possessed by demons, it has not been scary. The Holy Spirit has moved through the gifts of discerning of spirits and word of knowledge, and they got free.

Throughout my adult life, I have prayed as I approach each new year. Several years ago, as the new year was upon me, I prayed that every spiritual gift within me would be sharpened.

On Christmas Eve, during the communion service, I took communion, and then I sat down in the pew that was upfront and in the center section. I was at my daughter's church, and I did not know the people very well, having only briefly met a few of them. As the people walked by me after they took communion, I suddenly knew how many of the people felt as they walked in front of me. I did not read their minds, but I knew which ones were carrying loads, although their outward appearances did not show this. I was discerning what was within them. The gift we call the discerning of spirits discerns demon spirits, a true move of the Holy Spirit, and the souls (the part of each human which contains mind, will, and emotions) of humanity. Since this time, I have noticed when a person sits near me for a while, that I may start picking up on things like that. Sometimes, I begin to know the heart of a person in my midst.

On another occasion, I had to sit very near to a person at a crowded table, which required that I had to move back into a crowded corner beside a young man who always seemed to be coping with life quite well. However, the longer I sat beside him, the more I realized the deep despair of his soul. Later, a member of his family told me of the deep depression he had been experiencing. This gift continues to work at times in similar circumstances.

I enjoy this gift much more when I am discerning a true move of God. Of course, it also works to give a check on my spirit when something is not from God. Even so, I am careful not to speak against something that might be from the Holy Spirit.

What does God do when two prayers have been prayed by the same person but are exactly opposite? When I was young, I had prayed that God would not let me see any of the scary stuff, but I later prayed that God would sharpen every gift. Well, in this case, God went with the prayer that was prayed much more recently that was aligned with the current desires of my heart. The prayer for my spiritual gifts to be sharpened overrode the prayer to keep me out of all the scary stuff. Once a person makes progress in the spiritual journey, God considers that the person is a work in progress and does not keep all the words spoken as though they are set in stone. We are allowed to grow as we speak new words of faith.

I went into a business office a few months after the Christmas Eve communion service. My only thought was to conduct business. It may have been on a Sunday when I had an appointment with the businessman in his office because no one was in the office except this man, myself, and my husband, who had gone back to use the bathroom and stayed longer than I would have liked.

As I sat there, looking across the desk at the businessman, I saw a mask appear over the top half of his face, and I saw this with my natural eyes. I saw the man's lips twist into a sneer.

The mask covered a little bit more than the Lone Ranger's mask, but it was not solid black like the Lone Ranger's mask. It looked like the mask of an idol that I had seen in history books. I knew from the pictures, and I knew in my spirit that this was a mask of Baal. Through the Holy Spirit, I knew that this man had contact with the demon presence behind the idol. I was sensing its presence as I sat there, trying to discuss my business concerns.

Before this day, I had quickly discerned there was something unusual—not quite right about him, but this was because of general discernment before I zoomed in with detail as the gift of discerning of spirits became active. Sometimes, you sense something is happening out there is no vision with your natural eyes. There are degrees of spiritual insight as the gift of discerning of spirits operates.

The gift of word of knowledge works in tandem with the gift of discerning of spirits in my own life, and it can be hard for me to know which one is working at times. The gifts can bump into each other fast, so we just flow with them. We can submit to being a vessel for the Holy Spirit to move through, and we are free to reject the opportunity if we choose. We have free will. However, no one manages God. If we submit to Him, the Lord moves in ways that will surprise us.

I could not leave the business office with that thing manifesting and with my husband still in the building. So, I stayed and discussed business details until my husband was ready to leave, and I got him out of there as quickly as possible. I was not there very long but much longer than I would have liked.

Of all spiritual gifts, the discerning of spirits seems to be the one people need help with the most. I have counseled people with this gift because I have compassion for those who must learn to carry it.

A woman told me she had prayed for this gift of discerning of spirits, and it started working in a powerful way. I cannot imagine why anyone would pray for this gift unless they had a moment of zeal and asked to move in all the gifts. That happens! She contacted me to find out how she could send it back. I had to deliver the unwanted news that the "gifts and calling of God are without repentance" (Romans 11:29). After they emerge, there is no sending them back. The gifts may go dormant in certain circumstances, such as backsliding or being unwilling to move in the gifts. In some cases, gifts do go dormant, but they do not go away until we enter eternity.

Years earlier, when I learned that a young woman had the gift of discerning of spirits beginning to manifest, I became concerned. I felt she might have trouble learning to carry this gift. I do remember telling her that this gift is the hardest to bear. I wish I had known more, and I wish I could have been closer to her. Her mentor had died, and I suppose there was not another to rise to take her place. I talked to her a few years ago, and she was no longer serving the Lord. Of course, God may yet intervene in her life.

The gifts are a blessing after we learn to flow with them. Gifts tend to come forth when situations cannot be remedied through natural means. As wonderful as they are, they only work sporadically. Gifts rise quickly, and they can be impressive because God Himself is impressive, even when He only releases a smidgen of His power.

However, the fruit of the Spirit is something that builds as we walk with the Lord. The fruit of the Spirit is with us constantly as we allow the Lord to guide our lives. "The fruit of the Spirit is love, joy, peace, longsuffering, gentleness, faith, meekness, temperance: against such there is no law" (Galatians 5:22–23). The gifts come in to help in certain instances and in crisis moments, and they can be powerful in taking things in a new direction. The fruit is there as a steadying influence all the time. I love to be around Christians who have spent years in obedience to the Lord, and they are like fruit trees you can pick from to be strengthened and refreshed.

Apostle Paul taught about the gifts in 1 Corinthians in chapters 12 and 14, and right in the middle of all this teaching in operating in the gifts, he took an entire chapter to teach on the choicest of the spiritual fruit in the love chapter, which has become one of the most beloved chapters in the entire Bible. "But covet earnestly the best gifts: and yet shew I unto you a more excellent way" (1 Corinthians 12:31). First Corinthians, chapter 14, tells of the importance of the fullness of the Spirit in the church, a church abounding in fruitfulness and gifts. "Follow after charity (love), and desire spiritual gifts…" (1

Corinthians 14:1). Paul spent quite a lot of time teaching about life in the Spirit. The thought that we would try to live our Christian lives totally in the natural realm was not the model of Christianity that Paul presented to the church. Paul's revelation was one of a church filled with power.

The gift of healing springs up when someone is sick, and the gift of word of knowledge is voiced when people don't know what to do. A spiritual gift will rise to meet a human need. Although the gifts can be impressive, they are also practical.

My grandmother apparently had the gift of discerning of spirits. She usually knew if someone told the truth or not. I told the truth and remained in her good graces. My grandmother was a devout Nazarene, and she believed in "praying through" on a matter. When she would sense that there was something wrong in her family, she would pray with her neighbor who lived on a farm nearby; years before, "prayer partner" was a known phrase in the Christian community. They usually could pray through, and all would be well, but when they could not, something would occur in her family.

Just as dreamers and visionaries have made their way into my life for some time, about five and a half years ago, gifted ones began to find their way into the inbox of my phone. The memory of trying to figure out how to move in my own ministry was firmly imprinted. When I saw others reaching out for my help, I did not want to turn them away. My heart went out to them.

I see these gifted ones churning out solutions for mankind as they allow the Holy Spirit to move through them. They are precious souls who will release Father's solutions for other precious souls.

Hannah from South Korea is one of these gifted, precious souls. She has been bringing some of her dreams and visions to me for a while, and I have been helping her to understand the more symbolic ones. Hannah recently told me of seeing lightning against a pink background with her spiritual eyes. This happened when she was speaking into her wounded soul, which had been traumatized as a child. As she spoke words of healing and comfort to the traumatized "child Hannah," she felt comforted. She felt darkness lose its grip on her soul, and as she felt this release from the dark hold of oppression, she saw the lightning flash against the pink background. Then she felt a greater degree of freedom than she had ever known.

Why did the lightning flash with the pink background? And why was she able to see this with her spiritual eyes? Wasn't it enough to get free? What was the purpose of the pink lightning? These are my thoughts on the subject: Pink is the symbol of femininity, and I believe it was a symbol of her female soul. Many times, a newborn baby girl will be dressed in a pink dress to be taken home from the hospital. This delicate, pink dress shows the love and care her parents are clothing her in as they take her to her family home. Hannah was not wanted by her parents from the very beginning, and the emotional abuse went on and on through the years. I believe Heavenly Father gave Hannah that pink lightning to assure her that He is doing a quick and powerful work in her feminine soul. Also, the lightning banished the darkness as light always does.

Hannah says,

> Before I saw the pink lightning, I saw in my mind—demons being angry as if they were losing hold of

me, and I wondered if I had imagined it. Then I saw the pink lightning, and I saw it clearly in my spirit. Then I knew I was not just imagining it. Then I felt neutral and wondered what that lightning was. I do feel less tormented after that happened. I just saw the sky open up, and lightning flashed against a pink sky.

Hannah says she did not hear thunder. As God was healing her from trauma, He sent lightning with a gentle, pink sky. He gave her the light without the frightening thunder. Hannah continues in her healing journey toward total wholeness. She works with a therapist in her town, and she continues to schedule appointments to work toward her goal. In a lengthy, healing process, the experience with the pink lightning does appear to be a momentous time when she was able to advance, making the rest of her journey possible. She is taking the healing process by faith and says that this matter is settled as she believes in total wholeness.

The Lord speaks to Hannah about events in the nations of the world. As an intercessor, she prays and sometimes fasts about the warning visions God shows her. She tells of a time when she saw turmoil in Jerusalem and prayed for the peace of Jerusalem. She prayed for two days under a great spiritual burden until the ceasefire came. She tells of sensing thunder over Jerusalem in her spirit as she was praying. She did not hear the thunder, but she said that she "sensed the thunder."

One day, Hannah asked Jesus to tell her His favorite day on earth. Jesus simply answered, "When I was on the cross."

Hannah had grown up being threatened with the fear of hellfire, not healthy teaching about heaven and hell, but the constant threatening of hell. This was a part of the emotional abuse she endured as she was growing up.

Heavenly Father gave her a glimpse of the glory of heaven one day. She just looked up, and there it was! "I saw it like a flash in the sky. Cynthia, I know you call these 'snapshots.'" I know very well about the snapshots since many of my visions have been for just a moment.

They can appear for one second but be imprinted on the memory for a lifetime. God allowed Hannah to have a snapshot of heaven with her natural eyes.

Hannah says that she was having coffee with a friend as they sat at a table outside. She looked up in the sky and saw a few golden buildings. She says they were pure gold and clear. Hannah says there was a lot of light, light that was life-giving. She was given understanding that she saw an eternal kingdom.

Hannah speaks of a knowledge of this place as though she had a memory of it, and this is a mystery to her. She felt the comfort of home that she had craved all her life. Hannah told me that she gets teary-eyed when she thinks of this place, and she thinks of it often.

She says, "I also felt color vibration in the atmosphere of heaven's sky—like there's music. I felt the sense of an adventure in heaven—you know, like the way you feel when you're a kid." Hannah was willing to tell her story, hoping that others would learn of our benevolent God. She wants the world to know that God is not abusive, even though some people are.

I wanted to know things from an earthly perspective, but her answers did not always match my questions. How can you confine a description of heaven to earthly terms? You cannot.

I asked, "What was the color of the vibration of heaven that you saw?" This was her answer: "It's colorful, and there's music in a moving way, and I sensed that the atmosphere of heaven is all alive." She went on to tell me of a dream she had about heaven: "Once, I was imagining what it would be like to meet my Creator one day. That light, I had a dream of seeing the emerald, green Northern Lights. Later, I found in Scripture where there is an emerald rainbow around God's throne."

"And he that sat was to look upon like a jasper and a sardine stone: and there was a rainbow round about the throne, in sight like unto an emerald" (Revelation 4:3).

On another occasion, as she was meditating upon the Lord, she saw sapphires being poured out close to her by God's own hand. She wondered about this, and a few weeks later, God led her to this Scripture from Exodus 24:10, "And they saw the God of Israel: and there was under his feet as it were a paved work of a sapphire stone, and as it were the body of heaven in his clearness."

As I have listened to Hannah's story, I have learned that God is able to move through His anointed yet broken vessels. He does not wait until a person is fixed, but He moves through them, even as He is restoring them. As Hannah was having these spiritual experiences, she was undergoing trauma therapy with a professional therapist.

As I meet more gifted ones, I am amazed at the range of religious backgrounds. God calls them from all kinds of perspectives. Methodist, Baptist, Nazarene, Assembly of God, Lutheran, and non-denominational backgrounds. Some of them really enjoy connecting with the prophetic community, but others prefer to stay in their mainline denominations where they are comfortable with the doctrine.

Hannah is a high school economics teacher who designs jewelry and sells it in her spare time. She especially loves to create gold jewelry, which may explain why God gave her a glimpse of the gold buildings in heaven.

I find Hannah's story to be so interesting I will tell a bit more about her observations and reflections. Hannah has had a full range of spiritual dreams and visions, from the gold and glory of heaven to viewing the dark side of the spirit realm. She has had warning dreams that have sent her into burdened intercessory prayer. Hannah and I both believe that her time in travail in prayer lessened the effects of what she saw in her visions.

When Hannah was living in Thailand, she was driving her scooter when she saw the spirit of Ganesh up in a tree. Ganesh is one of many Hindu gods, and you may have seen this one in pictures, the one that resembles an elephant. He is revered by Hindu intellectuals, bankers, scribes, and authors. He is worshipped before these professionals launch major enterprises in their careers. Of course, when God has allowed Hannah to see such things with her natural eyes, she has followed through with prayer and spiritual warfare.

It has been interesting to trace some of the family lineages of these gifted ones. Many times, I have been able to go back and find some gifted or dedicated Christian in the family line. When I shook other family trees, I could not find any who had gone before them in an outstanding, noble nature. This has caused me to believe that I have been meeting some Abrahams who were at the very beginning of God's desire to work through a certain family line of spiritual distinction. These Abrahams seem to have been called by the sovereign will of God for reasons unknown to us. It is also possible that these individuals had great spiritual hunger, which does draw the Lord's presence like a strong magnet.

In Hannah's family line, there was a grandfather who had been martyred for his Christian faith during the Korean War. Obviously this level of dedication brought favor to the family, and this favor rest upon Hannah in the form of prophetic gifting. Although her parent identify as Christians, she says she never saw the nature of Christ in them. The family blessing does rest upon Hannah. Almighty God i the most astute bookkeeper in the universe, and nothing gets past him. Our great God has a sense of justice that extends to individuals, families, cities, and nations. God is not in a hurry. He waits for the right people to be born into the world to carry out His plans.

When I was young, I noticed patterns of God's blessing, and I have continued to trace blessing and favor. I noticed a young woman with an unusually beautiful voice. At nineteen, her voice was developed and mature like one would expect of a woman of thirty-five or so. I sat by this young woman in church whenever I could. I wondered why her voice was so outstanding.

One day, I was talking to this young woman's mother, and her story bubbled forth like a spring, with no questioning from me. God wanted me to hear the narrative. At age five, the singer's mother had lost her father to a sudden death. She had planned her own death, got on her pony, and was about to rush out in front of a fast-moving vehicle. Then she heard the audible voice of God, "Do not kill yourself. I have a plan for your life. I want you to grow up and marry and have children. Your children will grow up and serve Me in a mighty way."

Ah! This explained it. Heavenly Father had planned this voice long ago. I did not know this family well, but I did know that this family had been devout for generations. Her singing was such a blessing in our church. She was Father's gift to us every time she sang.

These love notes from heaven are sent to us and through us. When the Lord called out to the five-year-old girl when she was riding her pony, His voice was the channel for the love note. God was also sending love notes in the form of three children who would have an impact on the world.

God has been sending some of His love notes to Merrian in Florida. He communicates with her to warn and encourage others, as well as to help her with her own life. Merrian has been encouraging pastors in third-world countries as she prays with them and shares her visions with them.

Some of her visions involve international matters, and she prays for the nations. There are several visionaries with whom I communicate who have no interest in politics or world events, yet they are given information about things that are happening behind the scenes. Because they have little knowledge of world events, their visions and dreams amaze me. Their information comes forth by the Holy Spirit. Their dreams and visions are filled with symbols and literal details of global conflict and other matters looming over the horizon.

Before Merrian came into the level of spiritual perception she now has, she had an interest in paranormal phenomena that she later renounced. At one time, she became interested in unidentified flying objects, and she began to do research on the subject. She now believes that because of the UFO obsession, she had to fight some battles that she would otherwise not have had to fight. She tells of one such event when her house was invaded one night by a baseball-sized orb.

According to Merrian,

> The orb was evil, dark, rusty colored with other colors mixed in. I saw it in my son's bedroom when he was sleeping. The evil orb was making noises— kind of like mechanical sounds and hovering over my son. The evil orb made the noise, and then it lit up the entire room. It stayed bright for a moment, then it disappeared.

After the orb left, Merrian realized she needed to pray. She rebuked it in Jesus' name.

Later on, after Merrian had renounced her fascination with UFOs, she saw an orb that was of a positive nature. She was at work as a night watchman when a large orb appeared in front of her. It was twice the size of a beach ball. Just as suddenly as it appeared, it disappeared. She says that it came close to her but not too close.

Merrian said,

> The good orb did not make sounds. It was a deep shade of blue. When I looked into it, it was like I was looking deep into something. It was colorful and alive inside with energy. Very beautiful. I knew it was sent with revelation. Before that time, I had not begun to have visions, but after I looked into the blue orb, I began to have visions and revelations.

The deep blue orb was sent with revelation inside, and it was a harbinger of the revelation that would unfold in Merrian's life. Looking into the orb released this gift of revelation.

Merrian's gift has been increasing. I believe this gift will increase more and more, and Merrian concurs. Merrian greatly desires to properly understand her visions and dreams. It has been a joy to walk with her and work with her to unravel the riddles. When I see Christians with a lot of ability in one area and practically none everywhere else, I have learned to be patient. They are as Father has made them. I recognize that God has appointed His people to certain places in the church.

Merrian has a lot of ability to receive revelation, but sometimes she needs my help to interpret what she receives. I received some criticism a few weeks ago when a woman told me that everyone can interpret all their own dreams and visions and that a third-party interpreter is never needed! I had to laugh. There is a human tendency to want to be completely self-sufficient and work as a one-person ministry team. However, God created the members of the church to work together. God will not share His glory with any man or woman. If there arises a "man of the hour" with all eyes turned to him for the answer, human beings have a propensity to worship the human.

The Lord has given us synergistic means of ministry where we all need each other. I have thought about how efficient it would be if God gave me all the visions and dreams that I interpret instead of working with people all over the world, but God does not seem to be that concerned with efficiency. As I think of this matter of efficiency, I am reminded that efficiency plans have decreased interaction in the church, which was not Father's plan. God moves upon different visionaries in different ways, and He speaks to them on different subjects. I take all of this into consideration when I interpret. I not only look at the information, but I also look at the way God continues to move upon each visionary with the messages He wants to release to the Covenant children. If God gave all the information to me directly, I would miss out on the ways God works through others, and I would miss the sweet fellowship and joy. Father leads us with His wisdom, and we submit to His lead.

Tricia from New Mexico says, "I know my dreams came from the Lord because they were symbolic and too complicated for an eleven-year-old, which is when they began." Tricia grew up in a boarding school, and some of the students made her life almost unbearable with various forms of bullying.

One night, Tricia had a strange dream. She said,

> There was a wooden signpost that had two wooden
> boards hanging from it in the desert. There were
> pictures of two of the school kids on the boards
> hanging from it. One of their chains broke, and I
> woke up.

As time went on, that student left school and came back a bit
later. She must have enjoyed having a break from the bullying of that
student. She continued,

> I didn't think anything of it until I had another
> dream. It was the same signpost, only two different
> pictures were on the signs, and the chains of one
> broke completely, and the picture fell into the dirt.
> That student left the school and never came back.
> This happened a few times more, and I started to
> recognize a pattern.
> Then one night, I had a dream of the signpost
> again—only the pictures were of my mom and dad.
> My dad's chain broke, and his picture fell into the
> dirt. I woke up and ran to my parents' bedroom and
> told my mom I was worried about their marriage.
> She told me it was just a bad dream. I hoped she was
> right, but a week later, my father moved out, saying
> he was going to visit my grandmother because she
> was ill.

Her father did not come back. This dream was accurate, as the
others had been. His chain had broken, and his ties to the family
were severed forever. "Later, I found out my parents were getting
a divorce. God was preparing me for what I could not have seen
coming without the dream. This was something major in my life."

Without the dream, this traumatic event would have been even more emotionally devastating. The dream signaled that something was about to happen and buffered the jolt a bit.

Tricia tells how God has continued to communicate with her in her dreams:

> A few years later, I had a boyfriend, and I had another dream. This time, there was a great white oak tree next to the signpost, and it had a picture of my boyfriend on it. His chains did not just break, they blew up, and his sign flew into a million splinters that all landed in the oak tree. The splinters sucked the life out of the tree, and the tree turned black. Roses bloomed from the tips of the splinters, and the splinters wilted and died.

The relationship with her boyfriend ended, just as the dream had predicted. Tricia believes that in this symbolic dream, she was the tree, and the relationship would have been destructive if it had not ended. Again, I believe the dream helped her to be able to accept the situation, as had happened before.

Even though the dreams had helped her in the past, Tricia became afraid of the dreams, so she asked God to stop sending them. God answered her prayer, and the dreams stopped.

According to Tricia,

> I didn't get any more dreams until I asked for them again after I had married. When the dreams began again, they were different. They were no longer symbolic with signposts, but my dreams are now short snippets of the future.

In Tricia's adult life, her dreams have become literal, but they continue to be prophetic. Now, she accepts her dreams as a part of God's will for her life, and they are a comfort to her, as they should be.

Brenda, a college professor from the Philippines, tells of a unique experience that happened as she was walking across the campus:

> One time, as I was walking across the campus, I saw many leaves of trees scattered on the ground. I live in the Philippines, so we only have a dry and wet season. We have a few leaves that fall to the ground but nothing like the autumn season in some countries. This started at the beginning of the "ber" months. The sight of fallen autumn leaves led me to sense that the season of my life was going to change. I had only seen autumn scenes in books, so this was new to me. True enough, after that autumn scene was shown to me with my natural eyes, there were changes in my life. My future is still changing from one season to another, but I know God will be with me. God holds every season of my life, and I hold onto Him.

What has fascinated me about Brenda's story is that God showed her something with her natural eyes that she had only seen in pictures. She said that they do have a few leaves falling, but nothing like the carpet of autumn leaves she saw in the vision. Brenda understood the vision, and this knowledge helped her to transition into the next phase of her life.

Dar from Florida tells us,

> I remember several times when a loved one passed
> from this world; when I would be praying and
> thinking about Scripture, the same thing would
> happen each time. I would smell a strong fragrance
> of roses in the room. It has happened several times,
> and it was always reassuring.

Cynthia from Maine relates this story to us,

> We were doing worship outside on our front lawn.
> I was singing and playing, then I looked up and
> saw the most beautiful angel wing...just one wing...
> but it was so beautiful. It spoke to my heart; God's
> angelic beings are ever-present, guarding over us and
> enjoying our worship of Jesus.

Father's love notes are sent in such a variety of ways. One angel,
a large group of angels, or in Cynthia's case, it was an edifying
experience to look up and see one angel wing. In 2016,

Linda from Oklahoma caught a glimpse of an angel reading a
book. Father sends all kinds of love notes.

Sandra of New Zealand says she heard the audible voice of God once. She also tells of tingling sensations on her skin when she prays for others and does spiritual warfare. Once the Holy Spirit comes over her body, she feels confident that her prayer is being activated in the spiritual realm. Concerning hearing the audible voice of God, she says this happened when she was pleading with God for direction in a work situation.

Sandra says that God's answer surprised her. I believe if God had spoken to her in her spirit without the audible voice, she might have dismissed the directive word as a strange idea. Upon hearing the audible voice of God, she heeded the words and moved in the right direction.

I have heard shofars in the realm of the Spirit, but I have not yet heard the audible voice of God. I once heard Father speak a warning in my spirit, and as He spoke, I felt thunder shake in my chest. I did not hear the thunder, but I felt it. As I felt the thunder, God's words were emphasized, and I have never forgotten them.

My mother told me of the first time she heard the audible voice of God. She had been feeling a stirring in her spirit about a mission trip to England. One day, she sat down at the kitchen table to pray for further direction. She said, "God, I need to know which place in England you want me to go to." Just after she prayed, she heard the audible voice of God say, "Sussex." Mama had to get a map. She told me she wasn't sure if Sussex were a town, a river, or just what it was. She discovered that Sussex is a county.

After this, Mama was in the hospital with her sister who was near death. A van load of English intercessors felt led by the Lord to stop at the little hospital in a remote Texas town. When they went into the hospital room to pray, Mama asked them where they were from in England, and they told her "Sussex." That was the beginning of Mama's overseas travels in the ministry and the beginning of hearing Father speak to her in an audible voice. For about twenty years after this, I would hear her say, "You know, He just whispered it in my ear." I realize that she had ongoing direction from Father as He whispered into one ear.

Linda from Connecticut gave her testimony about an eventful day in her life:

> It was a memorable day when I witnessed a shooting and a death. I was one of three who were in the tire company when the shooter appeared in the building. After hours of investigation, I was sitting down when I saw rainbow colors going straight across my hands and feet. The rainbow colors remained about ten minutes before they disappeared. As I was driving home after the incident, there was a car in front of me with bumper stickers. They read: "Have Faith," "Pray More," "Give Thanks," and "God Watches Over You."

Linda went on to say,

> It was a day when heaven watched over me; I had been only a few feet from the shooter. Apparently, he had come into the building with one agenda on his mind to shoot one of the workers, but things could have turned out differently.

Linda believes she understands what happened:

> I believe the rainbows represent a blessing twofold.
> The rainbow colors went straight across, not in an
> arc. I first saw the rainbow stripes appear on the
> underside of my left shoe, then on the right, then on
> both hands.I do believe it represented the Covenant
> I have with God. Two weeks before the shooting, I
> had to put down my dog, Toby. I had felt torment,
> wondering if I had made the right decision. Toby
> had been struggling with dementia.
> I believe the fact that the rainbow appeared on two
> feet and two hands represented the four paws of my
> beloved Toby. I felt peace after that, believing God
> gave me assurance that my Toby is waiting for me in
> heaven.

When I hear of others telling of their pets "crossing the rainbow ridge," I will always think of Linda and Toby.

I asked if she saw the rainbow stripes with her natural eyes. he told me this was an encounter she will never forget, and the nemory of it had carried her through some difficult times when she id not feel God's presence. (I suppose this means that Linda saw his with her natural eyes. When questioning about supernatural appenings, I have learned that natural questions do not always have orresponding answers as I would expect. Interviewing people who ave had supernatural experiences is different from my interviews ack when I was a newspaper reporter. I continue to learn as I pursue nformation from the Spirit realm.)

It's hard to predict when we will feel God's presence and when e will not. There have been times when I have greatly desired to hear from the Lord and to feel His presence, and there was no answer and no presence. The more desperate I have become to hear from God at times, the more difficult it became to hear. Sometimes, I have asked others to help me seek.

I was looking through my notes when I began to write this book. This is what I found: Sometimes, I do not feel God's presence, but today, I suddenly felt His presence as I was talking to my pastor's wife. As we were having lunch, she began to tell me details about the founding of the nation of Israel. As she spoke, I suddenly felt a powerful witness of the Holy Spirit. We remember these times when we want to feel His presence, but we do not. There is comfort in the memories of God's presence.

There are seasons of God's presence, but sometimes when we feel His presence or hear from Him, it seems to come out of nowhere. I receive a lot of quick answers, and I've noticed that many are immediate, before five minutes. (We do ask funny questions at times, as heaven looks on in amusement. I have walked all over my house, asking God to help me find my glasses, and they were snugly perched on top of my head!) There are times when we do not get answers when we would like.

We never know when a love note will fall from heaven. Father may ask us to carry love notes to others, such as gifts, cards, freshly baked banana bread, visits to shut-ins, phone calls, texts, words of knowledge, words of wisdom, encouragement, a ride to the doctor's office. There are many acts of kindness, random and otherwise, which do qualify as love notes from heaven.

There was a particularly hard time in my life, and situation were not favorable. I knew God needed some time to move in my circumstances. In the middle of my difficulties, Father sent women with gifts to cheer me as I waited for my situation to improve. A bo:

arrived from my daughter, who lived in another state. It was filled with chocolates, beautiful stationery, cute bears, and other lovely gifts. On the same day, a friend and her daughter-in-law drove into my driveway with boxes of sweets, treats, and more cute bears. I knew that Father's eyes were turned toward me.

In six months, a new opportunity opened to me. A new job in another state with lots of ministry possibilities flowed my way, and I embraced this opportunity. While I was waiting, the love notes were encouraging.

When we are trusting in the Lord, we need to trust Him to get it right. What if I had said, "What's with all the bears? What I really need is a better job and better circumstances. Why doesn't God help me?" It's at this point that I see people getting angry with God. God's timeline is not always our timeline. Also, it may take some time to move in situations to get them ready for the Covenant child who is praying fervently.

I knew God had not abandoned me, but I did not know when His answers to my prayers would manifest. The kindness of friends and family and boxes of gifts touched my wounded heart and brought hope. I continue to work from the premise that God is good. This brings hope, even in trying times.

I grew up hearing the old saying, "Don't look a gift horse in the mouth." This means you should not look in his mouth with a critical attitude. After all, the horse cost you nothing.

When Father sends a love note, it may not be everything you need, but it will be something you need. Accept it with thanksgiving. I do believe that our gratitude touches the heart of God, and it gives Him real joy.

Our walk with Almighty God is a trust walk. Some Christians like to keep a prayer journal with dates recorded of when they prayed certain prayers and when they were answered. I have heard that prayer journals are meaningful to those who keep them.

As I wait for answers to prayers, I find a trail of blessings strewn along my path. Today, after a year and a half of lock-down on our church dinners because of the pandemic, we got to bring our covered dish casseroles, and we had a splendid potluck dinner. There was more food than usual, more joy than usual. Father blessed us with a heavenly feast! There were love notes being passed around the room as we talked around our tables.

I hope you will find your love notes and be willing to pass along some of them to others. May joy dwell in you as you travel your path with love notes dropping from heaven as you journey on to your reward. May blessings overtake you along the way.

Bibliography

Holy Bible, The: Authorized King James Version. (Holman Bible Publishers: 1998).

About the Author

Cynthia Hightower is a former high school teacher who also taught as an adjunct instructor in a community college. She continues to work with young Christians as a mentor. Cynthia feels called as an encourager in the church, and she also has a desire to see revival cover the earth before the Lord returns.

CPSIA information can be obtained
at www.ICGtesting.com
Printed in the USA
LVHW081540190822
726377LV00016B/1458

9 781685 567011